TOSEL®

READING SERIES

STARTER

READING 3

ITC International TOSEL Committee

CONTENTS

About TOSEL®

TOSEL (Test of Skills in the English Language) was developed to meet the demand for a more effective assessment of English as a foreign language for learners from specific cultural settings.

TOSEL evaluates and certifies the proficiency levels of English learners, from the age of 4 through adulthood, along with academic and job performance results.

Background

- Other English tests are ineffective in accurately measuring individual abilities
- Overuse of US-dominated testing systems in diverse cultural and educational contexts in the global English language learning market

Functions & Usage

- Assessment is categorized into 7 levels
- Used as a qualification for academic excellence for school admissions
- Used as a test to assess the English proficiency in the corporate and public sectors

Goals

- Create an effective tool for assessing and evaluating the English skills of English language learners
- Implement efficient and accessible testing systems and methods
- Provide constructive and developmental English education guidance

TOSEL® Strength

LEVELED ASSESSMENTS

An established English test system fit for seven different levels according to learners' cognitive development

ACCURATE DIAGNOSIS

A systematic and scientific diagnosis of learners' English proficiency

EXTENSIVE MATERIALS

Supplementary materials to help learners in an EFL environment to prepare for TOSEL and improve their proficiency

SUFFICIENT DATA

Content for each level developed by using data accumulated from more than 2,000,000 TOSEL test takers delegated at 15,000 schools and academies

CLASSIFIED AREAS OF INTELLIGENCE

Content designed to foster and expand the strengths of each student, categorized by the eight areas of intelligence

CONTINUITY

A complete course of English education ranging from kindergarten, elementary school, middle school, high schoool, and up to adults.

HIGH RELIABILITY

A high reliability level (Cronbach's alpha: .904 for elementary school students / .864 for university students) proven by several studies (Oxford University / Modern Language Journal)

SYSTEMATIC & EFFECTIVE ENGLISH EDUCATION

Accurate diagnosis and extensive materials which provide a step-by-step development in English learning, according to the quality of each learner's ability

TOSEL® Level Chart

Seven Separate Assessments

TOSEL divides the test into seven stages, by considering the test takers' cognitive levels, according to different ages. Unlike other assessments based on only one level, TOSEL includes separate assessments for preschool, elementary school, middle school, high school students, and for adults, which also includes both professionals and college students.

TOSEL's reporting system highlights the strengths and weaknesses of each test taker and suggests areas for further development.

COCOON

Suitable for children aged 4-6 (pre-schoolers)

The first step in the TOSEL system, the test is composed of colorful designs and interesting questions to interest young learners and to put them at ease.

Pre-STARTER

Suitable for children aged 7-8 (1st-2nd grades of elementary school)

Evaluates the ability to comprehend simple vocabulary, conversations, and sentences.

STARTER

Suitable for children aged 9-10 (3rd-4th grades of elementary school)

Evaluates the ability to comprehend short sentences and conversations related to everyday situations or topics.

BASIC

Suitable for children aged 11-12 (5th-6th grades of elementary school)

Evaluates the ability to communicate about personal information, daily activities, future plans, and past experiences in written and spoken language.

JUNIOR

Suitable for middle school students

Evaluates the ability to comprehend short paragraphs, practical texts, and speech covering general topics and to participate in simple daily conversations.

HIGH JUNIOR

Suitable for high school students

Evaluates the ability to use English fluently, accurately, and effectively on a wide range of social and academic subjects, as well as the ability to use sentences with a variety of complex structures.

ADVANCED

Suitable for university students and adults

Evaluates the ability to use practical English required for a job or work environment, as well as the ability to use and understand English at the university level.

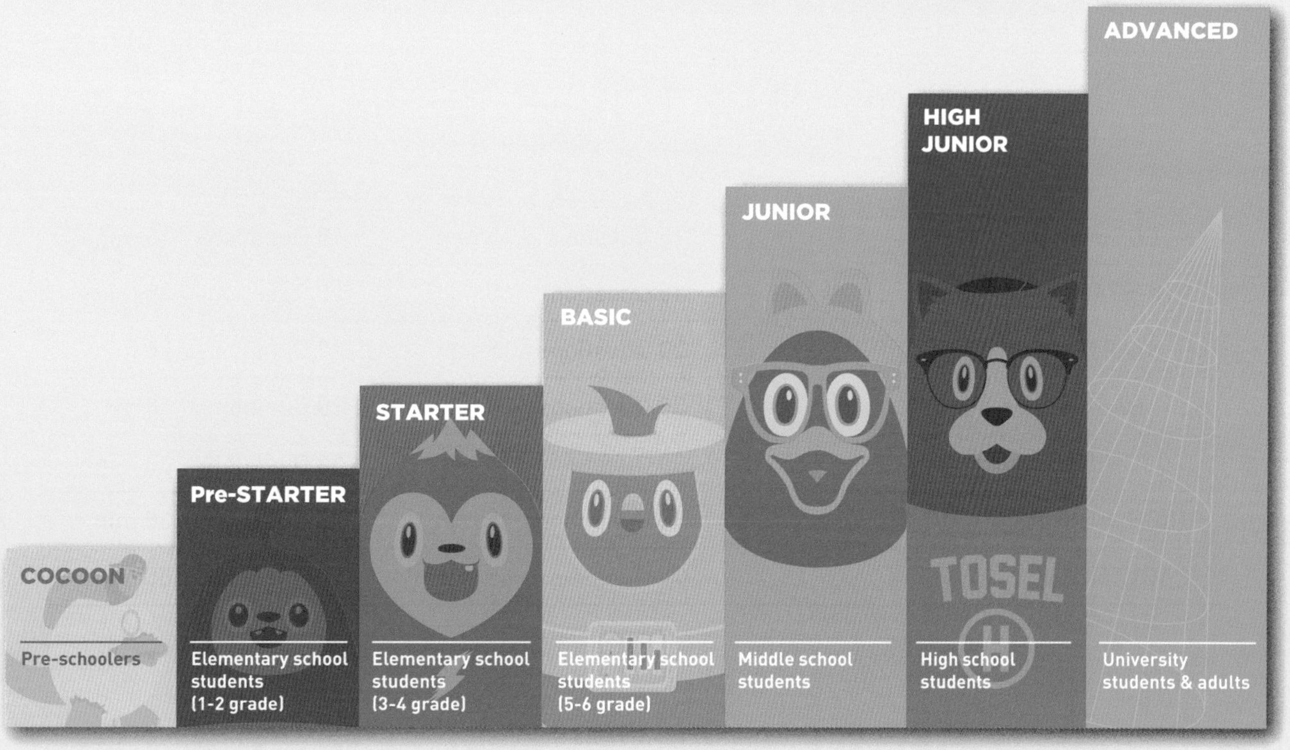

Evaluation

Assessing the Four Skills

TOSEL evaluates the four language skills: reading, listening, speaking and writing, through indirect and direct assessment items.

This system of evaluation is part of a concerted effort to break away from materials geared solely toward grammar and reading-oriented education.

TOSEL Test Information

Level	Score	Grade	Section Section I Listening & Speaking	 Section II Reading & Writing
COCOON	100		15 Questions / 15 min	15 Questions / 15 min
Pre-STARTER	100		15 Questions / 15 min	20 Questions / 25 min
STARTER	100		20 Questions / 15 min	20 Questions / 25 min
BASIC	100	1-10	30 Questions / 20 min	30 Questions / 30 min
JUNIOR	100		30 Questions / 20 min	30 Questions / 30 min
HIGH JUNIOR	100		30 Questions / 25 min	35 Questions / 35 min
ADVANCED	990		70 Questions / 45 min	70 Questions / 55 min

Certificates

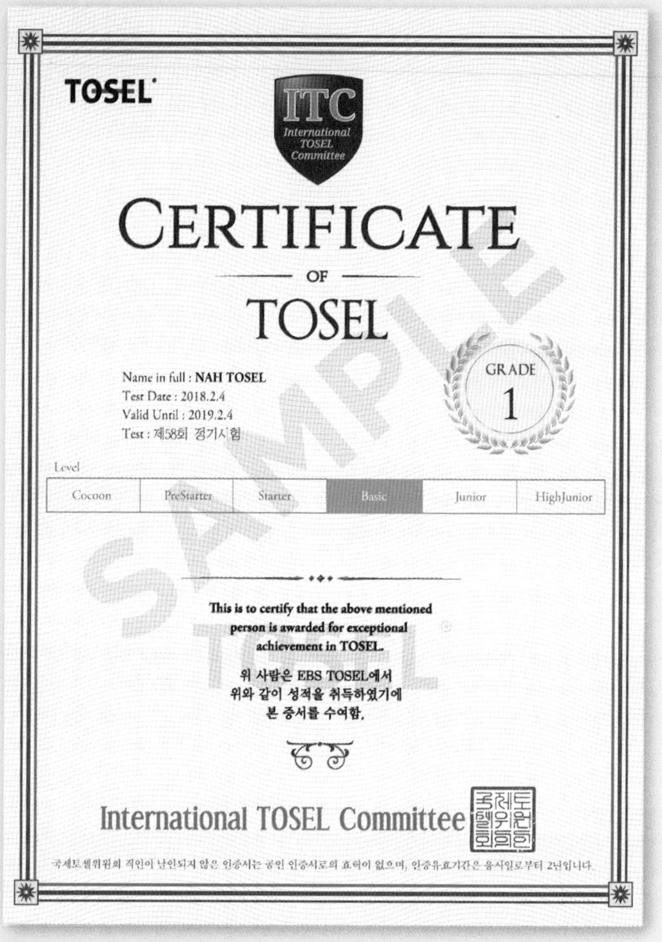

TOSEL Certificate

The International TOSEL Committee officially evaluates and certifies the level of English proficiency of English learners from the age of 4 to adults.

Certified by

Mar. 2010 Korea University
Dec. 2009 The Korean Society of Speech Science
Dec. 2009 The Korea Association of Foreign Language Education
Nov. 2009 The Applied Linguistics Association of Korea
Oct. 2009 The Pan Korea English Teachers Association

CHAPTER 1

School Activity

Teacher's Book
p.156

UNIT 1

Our Music Teacher

What sound does the violin make?
Can you make that sound?

UNIT 1 Our Music Teacher

My music teacher is very kind. Her name is Ms. Beesly. Every student likes her. Her class is very exciting. There are fifteen students in our class. Five students play the violin. Another five play the guitar. The last five play the flute. We play a beautiful song together. I play the violin. But I am not good at it. I get sad. After today's class, I talk to Ms. Beesly. I say, "I can't play the violin well. I'm bad at the violin!" Ms. Beesly smiles. She says, "Don't worry. I can help you." She helps me with the violin after school. Now I play the violin well. I like my music teacher!

New Words

kind

be good at

play

be bad at

Part A. Sentence Completion

1. Our teacher ________ a lot.

(A) smiles
(B) smiling
(C) is smile
(D) to smile

2. ________ you play the guitar?

(A) Is
(B) Can
(C) Has
(D) Does

Part B. Situational Writing

3.

She can play the ________.

(A) piano
(B) violin
(C) guitar
(D) trumpet

4.

There are ________ rabbits.

(A) five
(B) fifth
(C) fifty
(D) fifteen

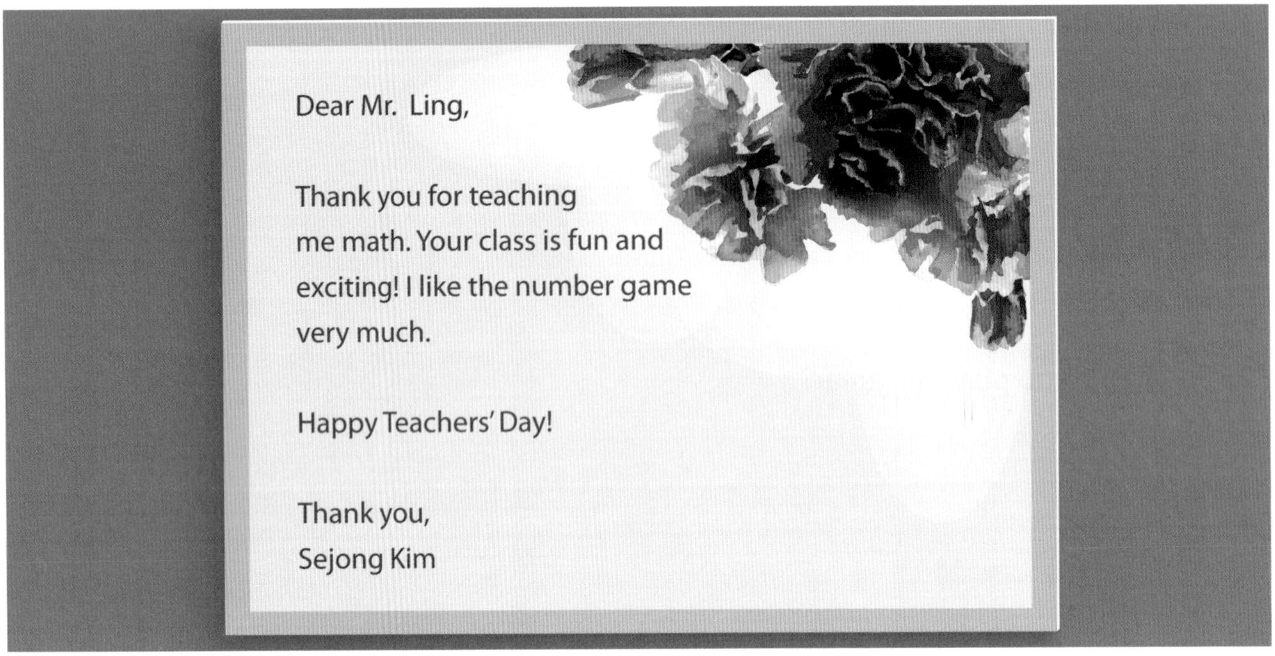

Dear Mr. Ling,

Thank you for teaching me math. Your class is fun and exciting! I like the number game very much.

Happy Teachers' Day!

Thank you,
Sejong Kim

5. Who is Mr. Ling, maybe?

(A) a math teacher
(B) Sejong's friend
(C) a music teacher
(D) Sejong's brother

6. Why does Sejong write the letter?

(A) for a birthday
(B) for Sports Day
(C) for Teachers' Day
(D) for a music contest

Part D. General Reading and Retelling

My music teacher is very kind. Her name is Ms. Beesly. Every student likes her. Her class is very exciting. There are fifteen students in our class. Five students play the violin. Another five play the guitar. The last five play the flute. We play a beautiful song together. I play the violin. But I am not good at it. I get sad. After today's class, I talk to Ms. Beesly. I say, "I can't play the violin well. I'm bad at the violin!" Ms. Beesly smiles. She says, "Don't worry. I can help you." She helps me with the violin after school. Now I play the violin well. I like my music teacher!

7. What is the best title?
   (A) My Beautiful Violin
   (B) The Bad Drummer
   (C) How to Play the Piano
   (D) My Great Music Teacher

8. What does the writer play?
   (A) the flute
   (B) the violin
   (C) the piano
   (D) the guitar

9. What is true about Ms. Beesly?
   (A) Her class is boring.
   (B) She teaches music.
   (C) Students do not like her.
   (D) She cannot play the violin.

10. How many students are in the class?
   (A) 5
   (B) 10
   (C) 15
   (D) 20

Listening Practice

Listen and write.

MP3 S3-1

Our Music Teacher

My music teacher is very [1] ________ . Her name is Ms. Beesly. Every student likes her. Her class is very exciting. There are fifteen students in our class. Five students [2] ________ the violin. Another five play the guitar. The last five play the flute. We play a beautiful song together. I play the violin. But I am not [3] ________ it. I get sad. After today's class, I talk to Ms. Beesly. I say, "I can't play the violin well. I'm [4] ________ the violin!" Ms. Beesly smiles. She says, "Don't worry. I can help you." She helps me with the violin after school. Now I play the violin well. I like my music teacher!

Word Bank

bad at	goodat
badat	kind
pray	good at
play	kend

Listen. Pause. Say each sentence.

MP3 S3-1G

Writing Practice

Write the words.

1

2

3

4

Write the words.

Summary

Ms. Beesly is a kind music teacher. In her class, students play the violin, the guitar, and the flute. I play the violin. I get sad because I ________________ the violin. Ms. Beesly is helping me.

Word Puzzle

B	E	B	A	D	A	T	Y	A	W	T	K	X	P	F
J	H	E	E	B	Y	Q	O	C	D	F	W	E	V	A
J	U	G	I	P	Z	T	U	Q	X	J	C	X	Y	G
Z	I	O	U	L	D	P	L	A	R	L	R	S	Q	O
S	F	O	F	A	F	C	M	R	Q	T	E	N	W	D
V	Q	D	G	Y	E	T	U	B	K	D	D	J	R	O
K	Z	A	Z	S	M	T	K	H	W	U	R	C	B	Y
I	M	T	C	H	P	V	B	T	T	L	P	P	O	R
A	Z	L	H	U	K	U	Q	Y	I	C	K	I	N	D
Z	Q	I	M	U	A	X	E	F	Q	I	B	E	Q	P
D	C	K	Z	U	L	C	N	Q	T	F	P	Y	L	K
U	P	L	U	Z	I	H	D	T	E	C	L	Q	G	U
V	I	F	G	D	H	U	P	F	D	C	Y	U	V	Q
A	U	L	G	X	S	F	Q	L	A	K	D	N	N	A
D	Z	M	J	Q	Y	E	N	G	C	E	V	G	K	C

Write the words. Then find them in the puzzle.

1 ______________

2 ______________

3 ______________

4 ______________

Teacher's Book p.160

UNIT 2

A Day at a Gallery

Think! You are at an art gallery.
What art can you see? Can you draw it?

UNIT 2 A Day at a Gallery

Eunji loves art. She loves to paint. And she loves to look at paintings. Eunji goes to an art gallery with her parents. The gallery is near her house. It is called Lux Art Center. She goes to the third floor first. Her favorite paintings are there. Her favorite artist is Lazio Sato. His art is famous. He paints strange pictures. One picture is called "Rich Life." In the painting, there is a deer. The deer has five heads and seven legs. The picture is strange. But it is beautiful. Eunji tries to touch the painting. A man runs up to her. He works in the gallery. He says, "You must not touch the artwork!" Eunji remembers, "I must not touch the paintings."

New Words

painting

gallery

touch

artwork

10 minutes

Part A. Sentence Completion

1. She ________ to paint.

(A) love

(B) loves

(C) loving

(D) to love

2. ________ at that painting! It is beautiful.

(A) Look

(B) Looks

(C) Looker

(D) Looking

Part B. Situational Writing

3. 

There is a ball ________ the toy horse.

(A) near

(B) under

(C) above

(D) behind

4. 

Let's go to the ________ today!

(A) zoo

(B) bank

(C) art gallery

(D) water park

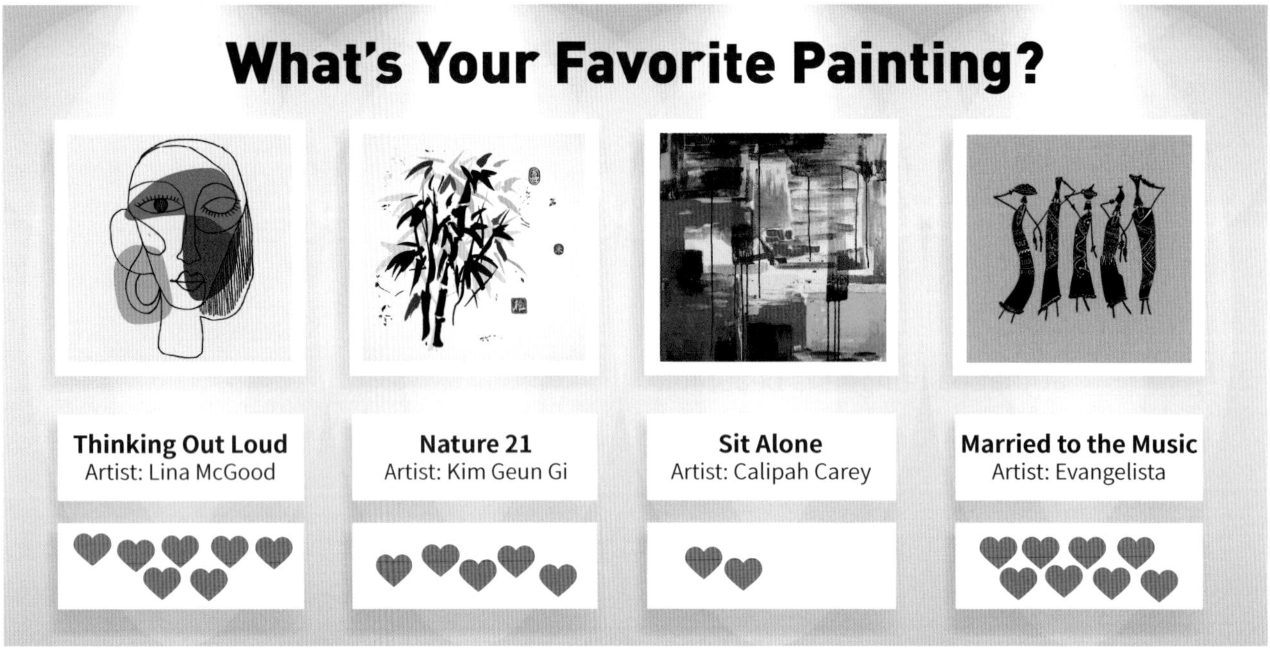

5. Whose painting is *Sit Alone*?

(A) Lina McGood
(B) Kim Geun Gi
(C) Calipah Carey
(D) Evangelista

6. Which painting do people like the most?

(A) *Thinking Out Loud*
(B) *Nature 21*
(C) *Sit Alone*
(D) *Married to the Music*

Part D. General Reading and Retelling

Eunji loves art. She loves to paint. And she loves to look at paintings. Eunji goes to an art gallery with her parents. The gallery is near her house. It is called Lux Art Center. She goes to the third floor first. Her favorite paintings are there. Her favorite artist is Lazio Sato. His art is famous. He paints strange pictures. One picture is called "Rich Life." In the painting, there is a deer. The deer has five heads and seven legs. The picture is strange. But it is beautiful. Eunji tries to touch the painting. A man runs up to her. He works in the gallery. He says, "You must not touch the artwork!" Eunji remembers, "I must not touch the paintings."

7. What does Eunji like to do?

(A) play the violin
(B) run in the park
(C) clean the gallery
(D) look at paintings

8. Who is Lazio Sato?

(A) Eunji's uncle
(B) a famous artist
(C) a restaurant chef
(D) Eunji's math teacher

9. What floor does Eunji visit first?

(A) 2nd
(B) 3rd
(C) 4th
(D) 5th

10. What is in "Rich Life"?

(A) a shiny ring
(B) a funny cow
(C) a strange deer
(D) a running man

Listening Practice

Listen and write.

MP3 S3-2

A Day at a Gallery

Eunji loves art. She loves to paint. And she loves to look at [1] ________. Eunji goes to an art [2] ________ with her parents. The gallery is near her house. It is called Lux Art Center. She goes to the third floor first. Her favorite paintings are there. Her favorite artist is Lazio Sato. His art is famous. He paints strange pictures. One picture is called "Rich Life." In the painting, there is a deer. The deer has five heads and seven legs. The picture is strange. But it is beautiful. Eunji tries to touch the painting. A man runs up to her. He works in the gallery. He says, "You must not touch the [3] ________!" Eunji remembers, "I must not [4] ________ the paintings."

Word Bank

galery	paintings
touch	gallery
toch	pentings
atwork	artwork

Listen. Pause. Say each sentence.

MP3 S3-2G

Writing Practice

Write the words.

1

2

3

4

Write the words.

Summary

Eunji loves to paint and look at ________________. She goes to an art gallery called Lux Art Center with her parents.

Word Puzzle

S	B	K	S	D	A	C	H	O	F	T	O	Z	P	T
Y	P	B	L	K	Y	L	V	X	Z	H	H	O	Q	O
S	Z	G	C	R	O	N	W	W	E	E	C	V	T	U
M	V	C	I	X	L	K	K	Q	H	H	N	R	F	C
B	Y	V	U	P	D	R	L	W	G	Y	R	W	L	H
D	F	W	P	A	G	U	R	S	G	Y	P	T	O	Z
E	S	O	Q	R	H	U	K	D	U	O	A	P	J	P
V	Z	R	K	E	Z	K	D	Y	Z	I	A	Y	T	U
S	Q	T	S	T	Z	W	B	X	B	M	A	B	U	D
Z	X	Q	T	Y	C	G	A	L	L	E	R	Y	Q	O
G	B	Y	Z	O	M	S	X	N	R	Q	T	N	E	I
P	A	I	N	T	I	N	G	D	S	H	W	C	C	R
N	Q	Y	G	Z	X	D	B	W	F	E	O	I	M	Z
U	H	Y	T	F	R	U	E	C	O	E	R	X	A	M
L	V	Y	H	M	G	Y	B	I	W	E	K	X	U	I

Write the words. Then find them in the puzzle.

1 ____________

2 ____________

3 ____________

4 ____________

Teacher's Book
p.164

UNIT 3

How Do You Make Salad?

You are making a salad.
What vegetables go in the salad?

UNIT 3 How Do You Make Salad?

Ava has a cooking class before lunch. Today, the class makes salad. Two students work together. The teacher chooses the groups. Ava works with Emma. Ava and Emma take out a large bowl. They put many vegetables on the table. They have tomatoes, cucumbers, black olives, and onions. The vegetables are very fresh. They are from the school garden. Ava cuts the vegetables. The teacher helps her. Then, Emma puts the vegetables in a bowl. She mixes them. Ava makes sour dressing with lemon. Emma puts cheese on the vegetables. Their salad looks great! They pour the dressing on the salad. They eat the salad with forks. They share the salad with other classmates. The cooking class is fun!

New Words

cucumber

sour

dressing

pour

Part A. Sentence Completion

1. The ________ are fresh!

   (A) vegetable
   (B) vegetables
   (C) a vegetable
   (D) my vegetables

2. Please ________ out a large bowl.

   (A) take
   (B) taker
   (C) takes
   (D) taking

Part B. Situational Writing

3.

Fresh salad is in a big ________.

(A) box
(B) bowl
(C) book
(D) basket

4.

Can you ________ some milk for me?

(A) mix
(B) pour
(C) cook
(D) dress

Part C. Practical Reading and Retelling

Salad Color Contest

1. Bring 3 vegetables.
2. Work together with one friend.
3. Together, make a salad with your vegetables.
4. Count the colors in your salad.
5. The winners have the most colors!

5. What does each student bring?

(A) salad
(B) a plate
(C) vegetables
(D) colored pencils

6. Who are the winners?

(A)

(B)

(C)

(D)

Part D. General Reading and Retelling

Ava has a cooking class before lunch. Today, the class makes salad. Two students work together. The teacher chooses the groups. Ava works with Emma. Ava and Emma take out a large bowl. They put many vegetables on the table. They have tomatoes, cucumbers, black olives, and onions. The vegetables are very fresh. They are from the school garden. Ava cuts the vegetables. The teacher helps her. Then, Emma puts the vegetables in a bowl. She mixes them. Ava makes sour dressing with lemon. Emma puts cheese on the vegetables. Their salad looks great! They pour the dressing on the salad. They eat the salad with forks. They share the salad with other classmates. The cooking class is fun!

7. What is the best title?

(A) Cooking Class
(B) School Garden
(C) Lemon Dressing
(D) Growing Vegetables

8. What do Ava and Emma make?

(A) onion soup
(B) fresh salad
(C) beef noodles
(D) tomato sauce

9. What flavor is the dressing?

(A) sour
(B) salty
(C) spicy
(D) sweet

10. What does Ava do?

(A) add cheese
(B) sew a dress
(C) buy potatoes
(D) cut vegetables

Listening Practice

Listen and write.

MP3 S3-3

How Do You Make Salad?

Ava has a cooking class before lunch. Today, the class makes salad. Two students work together. The teacher chooses the groups. Ava works with Emma. Ava and Emma take out a large bowl. They put many vegetables on the table. They have tomatoes, [1] ______________, black olives, and onions. The vegetables are very fresh. They are from the school garden. Ava cuts the vegetables. The teacher helps her. Then, Emma puts the vegetables in a bowl. She mixes them. Ava makes [2] ______________ dressing with lemon. Emma puts cheese on the vegetables. Their salad looks great! They [3] ______________ the [4] ______________ on the salad. They eat the salad with forks. They share the salad with other classmates. The cooking class is fun!

Word Bank

dresing	por
saur	cucumbers
pour	dressing
cocombers	sour

Listen. Pause. Say each sentence.

MP3 S3-3G

Writing Practice

Write the words.

1

2

3

4

Write the words.

Summary

Today, Ava and Emma make salad in their cooking class. They put vegetables in a bowl. They ________________ sour dressing on the salad.

Word Puzzle

K	M	V	Z	U	A	N	T	S	X	F	F	B	N	G
X	U	G	S	D	S	O	M	I	A	P	B	D	V	W
O	D	K	S	B	G	F	W	C	P	Y	B	N	K	S
X	R	O	P	U	G	Y	D	B	O	V	L	R	Q	O
K	E	Q	O	W	P	V	M	C	H	W	L	G	B	U
W	S	J	U	Q	R	L	W	N	T	R	E	X	O	R
A	S	H	R	S	Y	X	C	Y	R	R	L	J	R	N
L	I	V	D	G	X	J	U	C	N	Z	K	Q	G	B
F	N	E	V	A	A	R	C	C	B	L	W	N	K	F
U	G	U	S	B	R	R	U	C	U	K	J	G	W	N
T	E	F	N	R	H	W	M	U	X	M	F	T	L	X
T	R	J	B	G	A	B	B	P	P	F	I	Z	D	R
M	X	E	J	N	Y	Y	E	M	S	L	D	H	R	R
H	F	F	J	O	F	Q	R	X	I	Q	L	J	D	O
Z	O	I	H	A	U	D	I	N	H	K	I	I	T	R

Write the words. Then find them in the puzzle.

1 ____________ 2 ____________ 3 ____________ 4 ____________

Teacher's Book p.168

UNIT 4

A Book about Street Dogs

Do you like dogs? Think.
How can people help street dogs?

UNIT 4 A Book about Street Dogs

My reading buddy's name is Ariella. I am in Grade 3, and she is in Grade 6. On Mondays and Fridays, we meet in Ariella's classroom. She reads a book to me. I like books with many pictures. This week we read a book about street dogs. Street dogs do not have homes. They do not have owners. They live outside. Street dogs are very hungry. They sometimes cannot eat for many days. I tell Ariella, "There are many street dogs in our town!" She says, "Yes. Let's tell others about this." We try to help street dogs. We make posters. We write, "Dogs are your family! Please take care of them. Do not lose them."

New Words

buddy

street dog

owner

town

10 minutes

Part A. Sentence Completion

1. ________ dogs have no home.

(A) It
(B) This
(C) That
(D) Those

2. They ________ in the street.

(A) live
(B) lives
(C) a live
(D) living

Part B. Situational Writing

3.

The children play ________.

(A) inside
(B) outside
(C) in the kitchen
(D) in the classroom

4.

The dog and cat live in the ________.

(A) gym
(B) street
(C) house
(D) bakery

5. Who gets a notebook?

(A) Jake

(B) Abdul

(C) Cody

(D) Joao

6. What do the first place reading buddies win?

(A) nothing

(B) a backpack

(C) a set of markers

(D) a notebook

Part D. General Reading and Retelling

My reading buddy's name is Ariella. I am in Grade 3, and she is in Grade 6. On Mondays and Fridays, we meet in Ariella's classroom. She reads a book to me. I like books with many pictures. This week we read a book about street dogs. Street dogs do not have homes. They do not have owners. They live outside. Street dogs are very hungry. They sometimes cannot eat for many days. I tell Ariella, "There are many street dogs in our town!" She says, "Yes. Let's tell others about this." We try to help street dogs. We make posters. We write, "Dogs are your family! Please take care of them. Do not lose them."

7. What is the best title?

(A) My Pet Dog
(B) Fish and Other Pets
(C) Breakfast with Ariella
(D) Reading and Street Dogs

8. What does Ariella do?

(A) read books
(B) write stories
(C) care for cats
(D) teach French

9. What grade is Ariella in?

(A) 3
(B) 4
(C) 5
(D) 6

10. Why does the writer make a poster?

(A) to find a cat
(B) to win a contest
(C) to help street dogs
(D) to finish homework

Listening Practice

Listen and write.

MP3 S3-4

A Book about Street Dogs

My reading [1] ____________ 's name is Ariella. I am in Grade 3, and she is in Grade 6. On Mondays and Fridays, we meet in Ariella's classroom. She reads a book to me. I like books with many pictures. This week we read a book about [2] ____________ dogs. Street dogs do not have homes. They do not have [3] ____________. They live outside. Street dogs are very hungry. They sometimes cannot eat for many days. I tell Ariella, "There are many street dogs in our [4] ____________!" She says, "Yes. Let's tell others about this." We try to help street dogs. We make posters. We write, "Dogs are your family! Please take care of them. Do not lose them."

Word Bank

strit	buddy
oners	street
tawn	budy
town	owners

Listen. Pause. Say each sentence.

MP3 S3-4G

Writing Practice

Write the words.

1

2

3

4

Write the words.

Summary

Ariella reads books to me. This week we read a book about ______________ dogs, so I know about street dogs now. We try to help street dogs. We make posters.

Word Puzzle

H	R	K	O	H	G	F	R	D	V	T	O	S	Q	G
B	U	D	D	Y	A	S	X	K	D	C	T	O	W	N
H	O	E	Z	J	J	T	N	B	D	L	T	O	Y	V
V	W	O	W	N	E	R	V	W	J	Z	X	U	B	C
S	N	J	W	L	X	E	C	P	D	K	F	F	Q	W
R	H	H	P	O	Q	E	X	Z	Z	U	D	T	Y	N
T	R	R	V	Z	F	T	H	X	D	K	M	X	G	B
D	R	H	O	B	S	D	Z	K	O	M	K	R	C	H
M	M	Z	H	N	D	O	J	S	T	R	P	D	J	Z
I	R	V	J	X	B	G	I	S	M	A	F	Q	Y	N
X	B	U	W	A	D	R	C	C	M	K	V	C	V	L
U	Q	V	W	A	B	M	B	M	U	L	Y	D	F	Y
T	W	T	G	A	S	G	J	V	N	D	N	V	U	T
Z	S	X	J	B	T	T	L	N	F	D	E	M	I	I
G	W	U	C	Q	X	O	T	C	J	D	B	H	K	M

Write the words. Then find them in the puzzle.

1 ____________

2 ____________

3 ____________

4 ____________

CHAPTER REVIEW

Match the pictures to the correct words.

Teacher's Book
p.172

artwork

be bad at

be good at

buddy

cucumber

dressing

gallery

kind

owner

painting

play

pour

sour

street dog

touch

town

CHAPTER 2

School Festival

Teacher's Book p.173

UNIT 5

Field Trip to the Aquarium

These animals live in the ocean.
Which can you name?

UNIT 5 Field Trip to the Aquarium

We're going on a field trip. Where are we going? We want to see many fish. So we are going to the aquarium in our town! Look! There is a beautiful starfish. It really looks like a star. And look at those small fish! They are black and orange! They swim together. They are good friends. What is starting soon? It is the mermaid show. The mermaids are not fish. They are real people. They are divers. They wear costumes and dance to music. They wave to us. They are so great! We also touch turtles at the aquarium. They can go in the water and on land. We're all excited. We want to come to the aquarium again. When is the next field trip?

New Words

aquarium

mermaid

costume

wave

10 minutes

Part A. Sentence Completion

1. The turtles walk very ________.

(A) slow
(B) slows
(C) slowly
(D) slower

2. There are many ________ in my fish bowl.

(A) fish
(B) to fish
(C) my fish
(D) the fish

Part B. Situational Writing

3.

The ________ lives in the sea.

(A) turtle
(B) shark
(C) dolphin
(D) mermaid

4.

Martin is ________ to us.

(A) waving
(B) running
(C) jumping
(D) swimming

Aquarium Tour Schedule

9:30-10:00 AM	10:30-11:00 AM	11:00-11:30 AM	1:00-1:30 PM	1:30-2:00 PM
Drawing Starfish	Playing with Turtles	Mermaids Show	Feeding Turtles	Learning about Sharks

• Lunch Hour: 11:30 AM - 12:30 PM

5. What starts after lunch?

(A) Drawing Starfish
(B) Playing with Turtles
(C) Mermaids Show
(D) Feeding Turtles

6. What can you learn about at 1:45?

(A) frogs
(B) turtles
(C) sharks
(D) dolphins

Part D. General Reading and Retelling

We're going on a field trip. Where are we going? We want to see many fish. So we are going to the aquarium in our town! Look! There is a beautiful starfish. It really looks like a star. And look at those small fish! They are black and orange! They swim together. They are good friends. What is starting soon? It is the mermaid show. The mermaids are not fish. They are real people. They are divers. They wear costumes and dance to music. They wave to us. They are so great! We also touch turtles at the aquarium. They can go in the water and on land. We're all excited. We want to come to the aquarium again. When is the next field trip?

7. What is the best title?

(A) Stop Catching Fish
(B) Fun at the Aquarium
(C) Starfish Cannot Walk
(D) Cleaning the Aquarium

8. What is NOT in the aquarium?

(A) turtles
(B) lizards
(C) starfish
(D) mermaids

9. What do the mermaids do?

(A) sing songs
(B) play music
(C) read books
(D) wave to people

10. What does the writer touch?

(A) a turtle
(B) a squid
(C) an octopus
(D) an orange fish

Listening Practice

Listen and write.

MP3 S3-5

Field Trip to the Aquarium

We're going on a field trip. Where are we going? We want to see many fish. So we are going to the [1] in our town! Look! There is a beautiful starfish. It really looks like a star. And look at those small fish! They are black and orange! They swim together. They are good friends. What is starting soon? It is the [2] show. The mermaids are not fish. They are real people. They are divers. They wear [3] and dance to music. They [4] to us. They are so great! We also touch turtles at the aquarium. They can go in the water and on land. We're all excited. We want to come to the aquarium again. When is the next field trip?

Word Bank

cosstumes	wave
mermaid	wabe
aquarium	costumes
aquerium	mermad

Listen. Pause. Say each sentence.

MP3 S3-5G

Writing Practice

Write the words.

1

2

3

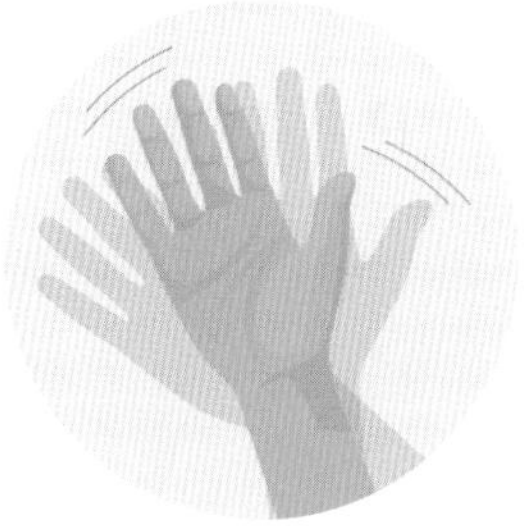

4

Write the words.

Summary

We go to the ________________ for our field trip. There are many fish.
There is also a mermaid show. We want to come back to the aquarium.

Word Puzzle

I	H	I	U	F	W	G	N	N	O	B	A	A	B	L
G	K	A	C	O	S	T	U	M	E	O	Q	G	O	H
W	V	O	N	E	H	I	V	S	F	P	U	V	B	E
A	R	L	E	A	H	T	G	L	F	G	A	B	H	T
V	T	G	M	E	R	M	A	I	D	U	R	C	E	C
E	A	D	R	H	S	Y	D	L	F	T	I	Z	K	R
V	K	Z	B	R	R	O	W	O	B	A	U	M	E	A
W	W	I	I	U	T	I	V	D	Y	F	M	F	U	N
N	L	N	F	Z	G	I	B	N	B	P	J	G	O	L
V	V	J	P	V	T	C	M	J	E	A	J	J	P	P
L	Y	A	R	L	U	Q	R	D	P	E	B	P	N	B
V	Y	N	U	S	K	E	J	Y	H	C	T	O	J	R
G	S	L	Z	M	G	L	B	R	M	Z	S	K	V	X
W	Z	A	S	T	X	A	S	L	C	Z	S	I	S	B
J	W	N	A	E	Q	R	K	S	V	Q	U	F	P	U

Write the words. Then find them in the puzzle.

1 ____________________

2 ____________________

3 ____________________

4 ____________________

Teacher's Book p.177

UNIT 6

The Book Fair

What is your favorite book?
What is it about?

UNIT 6 The Book Fair

Today is the book fair! Cora wants to buy a book about robots. She wants a book with nice pictures. Ron likes kings and queens. He wants a book called "English Kings." Ron can get a crown with the book. The school bell rings. Cora and Ron run to the library. The book fair is there. Cora looks for a robot book. She finds a book with many pictures. Ron looks for "English Kings." There is only one copy. Oh no! Lydia gets the book first. Ron is sad. He cries. Cora feels bad. She says to Ron, "Let's read my robot book together!" Cora and Ron read the book together. Ron is happy. It is a good book fair!

New Words

book fair

crown

king

queen

Part A. Sentence Completion

1. There ________ a red flower in the vase.

(A) is
(B) be
(C) do
(D) are

2. Ron shouts, "Let's ________ to a robot song!"

(A) dance
(B) dances
(C) dancing
(D) to dance

Part B. Situational Writing

3.

The queen wears a golden ________.

(A) ring
(B) crown
(C) helmet
(D) necklace

4.

The phone is ________ very loudly.

(A) turning
(B) ringing
(C) moving
(D) cooking

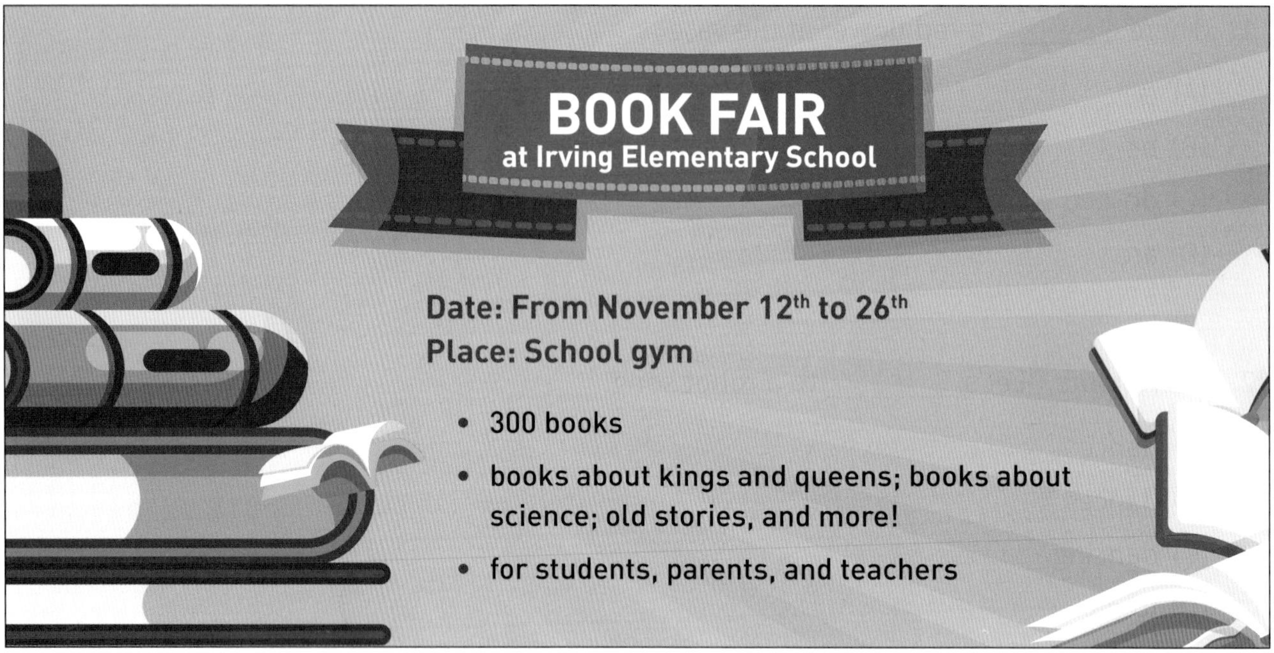

5. Where is the book fair?

(A) in a gym
(B) at a beach
(C) in a library
(D) at a museum

6. How many books are there?

(A) 100
(B) 200
(C) 300
(D) 400

Part D. General Reading and Retelling

Today is the book fair! Cora wants to buy a book about robots. She wants a book with nice pictures. Ron likes kings and queens. He wants a book called "English Kings." Ron can get a crown with the book. The school bell rings. Cora and Ron run to the library. The book fair is there. Cora looks for a robot book. She finds a book with many pictures. Ron looks for "English Kings." There is only one copy. Oh no! Lydia gets the book first. Ron is sad. He cries. Cora feels bad. She says to Ron, "Let's read my robot book together!" Cora and Ron read the book together. Ron is happy. It is a good book fair!

7. What is the best title?
   (A) Jumping at School
   (B) The School Book Fair
   (C) The Library Loses a Book
   (D) How to Make Robots at Home

8. When is the book fair?
   (A) today
   (B) tomorrow
   (C) next week
   (D) next month

9. What can Ron get with "English Kings"?
   (A) a bell
   (B) a robot
   (C) a photo
   (D) a crown

10. What do Cora and Ron do together?
   (A) wear crowns
   (B) take pictures
   (C) cry about books
   (D) read about robots

Listening Practice

Listen and write.

MP3 S3-6

The Book Fair

Today is the book [1] ________ ! Cora wants to buy a book about robots. She wants a book with nice pictures. Ron likes [2] ________ and [3] ________ . He wants a book called "English Kings." Ron can get a [4] ________ with the book. The school bell rings. Cora and Ron run to the library. The book fair is there. Cora looks for a robot book. She finds a book with many pictures. Ron looks for "English Kings." There is only one copy. Oh no! Lydia gets the book first. Ron is sad. He cries. Cora feels bad. She says to Ron, "Let's read my robot book together!" Cora and Ron read the book together. Ron is happy. It is a good book fair!

Word Bank

queens	crown
keens	far
fair	crawn
kings	kigns

Listen. Pause. Say each sentence.

MP3 S3-6G

Writing Practice

Write the words.

1 □□□□ □□□□

2 □□□□□

3 □□□□

4 □□□□□

Write the words.

Summary

Cora and Ron go to the ________________. Cora finds a robot book. Ron cannot get a book. He is sad. But Cora and Ron read the robot book together. Then Ron is happy.

Word Puzzle

Z	Q	Y	V	D	B	Q	G	U	Y	Y	V	G	O	S
Q	V	T	G	W	N	F	E	M	T	Y	P	N	B	S
D	T	C	H	G	O	I	A	N	V	U	B	V	D	I
V	V	X	Z	S	R	Y	L	L	L	B	W	J	X	O
H	X	E	J	F	X	F	T	M	Z	O	I	W	A	W
Q	X	P	K	O	V	I	Y	L	C	O	P	R	I	G
Y	U	B	G	Z	D	H	P	J	L	K	D	I	S	X
H	B	H	Z	C	K	C	B	L	A	F	J	I	N	I
H	H	V	S	M	I	D	N	N	T	A	Z	M	M	A
E	V	K	M	T	N	A	C	X	A	I	M	X	U	N
I	D	F	W	A	G	S	F	U	V	R	U	C	I	Z
P	E	R	O	R	O	Z	I	R	H	M	U	R	P	U
Y	O	H	K	G	B	K	B	N	B	U	K	O	T	D
X	U	R	Z	L	B	E	H	J	E	K	R	W	Q	B
Y	P	S	X	A	E	L	X	Q	U	E	E	N	Y	P

Write the words. Then find them in the puzzle.

1 ____________

2 ____________

3 ____________

4 ____________

Teacher's Book
p.181

UNIT 7

Fast Runners

Think! You and your best friend run.
Who is faster?

UNIT 7 Fast Runners

I am a fast runner in my class. But there is another fast runner. His name is Reo. Who is faster? We do not know. Everyone wants to know. Reo has long legs. But I am very strong. I want to be faster. Today is Sports Day at school. Reo and I are having a race. It is time to race! We stand on the start line. The teacher shouts, "Start!" The race starts! Everyone cheers. I run faster and faster. Where is Reo? He is behind me! But he runs faster and faster. Now he is in front of me! Who gets to the finish line first? The teacher says, "You are both the winners!" Who is faster? We still do not know!

New Words

fast

race

winner

finish

Part A. Sentence Completion

1. She is a fast ________.

(A) run
(B) runner
(C) running
(D) runners

2. ________ is faster? He is faster!

(A) Who
(B) Why
(C) What
(D) When

Part B. Situational Writing

3.

The green bag is ________ than the blue one.

(A) faster
(B) bigger
(C) slower
(D) smaller

4.

They ________ for the soccer players.

(A) win
(B) run
(C) start
(D) cheer

Part C. Practical Reading and Retelling

Run Like an Animal!

Choose your favorite animal, and run like it!
All students run together!

Do you want to be a cat? Then, you say 'meow' and run!
Do you want to be a cow? Then, you say 'moo' and run!
Do you want to be a pig? Then, you say 'oink' and run!

The winners get cute animal socks!

5. Tony runs like a pig. What does he say?

   (A) Moo!
   (B) Oink!
   (C) Bark!
   (D) Meow!

6. What do winners get?

   (A) socks
   (B) books
   (C) pet animals
   (D) cute erasers

Part D. General Reading and Retelling

I am a fast runner in my class. But there is another fast runner. His name is Reo. Who is faster? We do not know. Everyone wants to know. Reo has long legs. But I am very strong. I want to be faster. Today is Sports Day at school. Reo and I are having a race. It is time to race! We stand on the start line. The teacher shouts, "Start!" The race starts! Everyone cheers. I run faster and faster. Where is Reo? He is behind me! But he runs faster and faster. Now he is in front of me! Who gets to the finish line first? The teacher says, "You are both the winners!" Who is faster? We still do not know!

7. What is the best title?

(A) Do You Like Cars?
(B) Who Runs Faster?
(C) Who Hates Sports?
(D) Do You Walk or Run?

8. What day is it?

(A) Sports Day
(B) Car Race Day
(C) Book Club Day
(D) Science Fair Day

9. What does Reo have?

(A) long legs
(B) a fast car
(C) a magic hat
(D) special shoes

10. Who wins the race?

(A) Reo
(B) the writer
(C) the teacher
(D) both runners

Listening Practice

Listen and write.

MP3 S3-7

Fast Runners

I am a [1] ______ runner in my class. But there is another fast runner. His name is Reo. Who is faster? We do not know. Everyone wants to know. Reo has long legs. But I am very strong. I want to be faster. Today is Sports Day at school. Reo and I are having a [2] ______ . It is time to race! We stand on the start line. The teacher shouts, “Start!” The race starts! Everyone cheers. I run faster and faster. Where is Reo? He is behind me! But he runs faster and faster. Now he is in front of me! Who gets to the [3] ______ line first? The teacher says, “You are both the [4] ______ !” Who is faster? We still do not know!

Word Bank

finish	past
finnish	fast
lace	race
winners	winers

Listen. Pause. Say each sentence.

MP3 S3-7G

Writing Practice

Write the words.

1 ☐☐☐☐

2 ☐☐☐☐

3 ☐☐☐☐☐☐

4 ☐☐☐☐☐☐

Write the words.

Summary

Reo and I are both fast runners. Today we have a ____________________. The race starts. Everyone cheers. But who is faster? We do not know.

Word Puzzle

K	U	C	Z	R	J	K	M	W	P	I	Z	S	O	Z
U	A	K	Q	Y	X	G	M	I	B	T	G	O	F	K
Q	I	J	B	N	P	W	K	N	Z	S	V	L	K	G
N	P	T	F	P	H	E	L	N	Q	B	U	P	L	Y
J	G	X	H	N	X	I	W	E	G	E	W	I	O	W
C	W	O	X	V	F	H	R	R	M	H	D	R	H	W
F	Q	S	Y	Q	A	C	Z	T	U	J	J	W	L	D
T	W	W	D	S	T	D	M	E	P	O	P	V	L	J
I	F	O	U	E	H	C	R	W	F	P	J	W	V	K
Z	F	I	N	I	S	H	P	K	F	F	H	Z	R	S
L	I	F	O	R	A	V	Y	O	C	P	O	E	Q	N
K	Y	U	R	C	Z	D	X	W	X	W	R	P	S	A
P	G	A	T	Z	B	Q	V	Z	V	Y	A	E	N	N
N	D	F	Q	D	U	F	A	S	T	R	C	O	B	J
S	X	K	L	R	J	F	Y	N	J	H	E	M	F	C

Write the words. Then find them in the puzzle.

1 ______________

2 ______________

3 ______________

4 ______________

Teacher's Book p.185

UNIT 8

Buying and Selling

There is a market at school today.
What do you sell? What do you buy?

UNIT 8 Buying and Selling

Today is the school market. We can buy and sell things today at school! On the first floor, students sell toys and dolls. I see Minji. She is selling Russian dolls. They have smaller dolls inside them. They are cute! I buy two dolls for my parents. I go to the second floor. Students are selling old things there. I see Juan. He is selling a clock. The clock is old. But it works well. How much is it? 100 dollars? It is expensive. I cannot buy it. I go to the third floor. There, students are selling games. I put my board game on the table. Erika comes to me. She asks, “What is this game?” I say, “It is a board game about mermaids.” Erika buys it. Wow! I get 3 dollars!

New Words

market

sell

expensive

board game

Part A. Sentence Completion

1. What ________ these books?

(A) is
(B) do
(C) be
(D) are

2. Where are his books? ________ are on the table.

(A) It
(B) He
(C) She
(D) They

Part B. Situational Writing

3.

This chair is very ________! 200 years!

(A) old
(B) wet
(C) blue
(D) purple

4.

This is my new set of Russian ________.

(A) dolls
(B) clocks
(C) boards
(D) markets

Ports Elementary School Market

- When: November 22nd
- Where: Ports Elementary School 1st floor

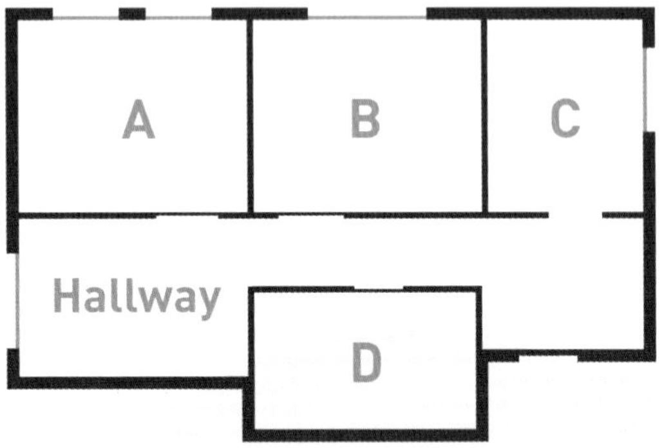

You can buy and sell:

- A: Books, pens, and notebooks
- B: New toys and dolls
- C: Old things
- D: Snacks and drinks

- All Ports Elementary School students can sell things.
- Please do not leave things in the hallway.

5. Where can you buy an old doll?

   (A) A
   (B) B
   (C) C
   (D) D

6. What can students NOT do?

   (A) buy food
   (B) go to the first floor
   (C) sell things to others
   (D) leave things in the hallway

Part D. General Reading and Retelling

Today is the school market. We can buy and sell things today at school! On the first floor, students sell toys and dolls. I see Minji. She is selling Russian dolls. They have smaller dolls inside them. They are cute! I buy two dolls for my parents. I go to the second floor. Students are selling old things there. I see Juan. He is selling a clock. The clock is old. But it works well. How much is it? 100 dollars? It is expensive. I cannot buy it. I go to the third floor. There, students are selling games. I put my board game on the table. Erika comes to me. She asks, "What is this game?" I say, "It is a board game about mermaids." Erika buys it. Wow! I get 3 dollars!

7. What is the best title?
   - (A) School Tour Guide
   - (B) A Horse Makes Dolls
   - (C) Buy and Sell at School
   - (D) A Bad Day at the Supermarket

8. What does the writer buy?
   - (A) nothing
   - (B) a clock
   - (C) Russian dolls
   - (D) a fairy tale game

9. What is true about Juan's clock?
   - (A) It works well.
   - (B) It is very cheap.
   - (C) Erika is selling it.
   - (D) Juan buys the clock.

10. What is on the third floor, maybe?
    - (A) old cups
    - (B) coloring books
    - (C) fresh tomatoes
    - (D) toy robot games

Listening Practice

Listen and write.

MP3 S3-8

Buying and Selling

Today is the school [1] ________. We can buy and [2] ________ things today at school! On the first floor, students sell toys and dolls. I see Minji. She is selling Russian dolls. They have smaller dolls inside them. They are cute! I buy two dolls for my parents. I go to the second floor. Students are selling old things there. I see Juan. He is selling a clock. The clock is old. But it works well. How much is it? 100 dollars? It is [3] ________. I cannot buy it. I go to the third floor. There, students are selling games. I put my [4] ________ game on the table. Erika comes to me. She asks, "What is this game?" I say, "It is a board game about mermaids." Erika buys it. Wow! I get 3 dollars!

Word Bank

sell	sel
bord	expensive
board	maket
iexpensive	market

Listen. Pause. Say each sentence.

MP3 S3-8G

Writing Practice

Write the words.

1

2

3

4

Write the words.

Summary

Today is the school ______________. We can buy and sell things at school. There are toys, dolls, old things, and games.

Word Puzzle

Y	S	H	L	O	I	G	U	H	I	M	Z	P	I	Q
A	O	W	I	V	W	E	X	P	E	N	S	I	V	E
N	S	P	M	Y	H	D	M	R	G	V	V	C	E	Y
B	L	Q	V	E	D	S	C	D	S	B	A	E	H	M
A	C	B	W	O	O	B	H	O	X	W	H	A	A	A
C	L	N	H	A	S	O	L	I	S	B	E	F	J	L
P	W	A	D	J	N	D	U	D	E	T	N	W	J	V
J	R	O	B	O	A	R	D	G	A	M	E	C	L	D
F	Y	E	F	J	B	J	H	P	L	G	Q	P	J	A
I	V	C	H	R	U	K	M	P	R	X	X	G	K	T
F	C	H	Z	U	M	A	R	K	E	T	B	T	P	H
T	G	A	W	H	L	A	Y	M	I	E	F	G	J	L
F	Z	A	M	F	K	S	E	L	L	Z	P	C	G	S
T	W	L	H	T	H	G	R	F	F	G	F	I	K	R
Z	B	D	H	F	R	N	V	V	M	P	E	H	M	G

Write the words. Then find them in the puzzle.

1 ______________

2 ______________

3 ______________

4 ______________

CHAPTER REVIEW

Match the pictures to the correct words.

Teacher's Book p.189

aquarium

board game

book fair

costume

crown

expensive

fast

finish

king

market

mermaid

queen

race

sell

wave

winner

CHAPTER 3

Fun with Friends

Teacher's Book
p.190

UNIT 9

My New Best Friend

Do you like reading with friends?
Who reads with you?

UNIT 9 My New Best Friend

Our class has a new student. Her name is Vicky. She is from another country. She looks shy. I am shy, too. Vicky sits next to me. At first, we do not talk. She and I are very quiet. I want to talk to her. Then, I see a comic book in her bag. It is "Mayo's Hamburger." It is my favorite story! I talk to her. I ask, "Do you like Mayo's Hamburger?" She says, "Yes! It is my favorite story!" Now, Vicky and I love to be together. We talk about comics at lunch. After school, we go to a comic book store downtown. There we read many funny comic books. We laugh for hours. Vicky is my best friend!

New Words

shy

comic book

funny

laugh

Part A. Sentence Completion

1. ________ do not talk.

   (A) It
   (B) We
   (C) He
   (D) She

2. I play soccer ________ lunch.

   (A) at
   (B) in
   (C) on
   (D) under

Part B. Situational Writing

3.

Can I borrow your ________ book?

   (A) card
   (B) paint
   (C) comic
   (D) movie

4.

The clock is ________ the bed.

   (A) on
   (B) under
   (C) above
   (D) next to

5. Mina spends one hour in the cafe. How much does she pay?

(A) 1 dollar
(B) 3 dollars
(C) 5 dollars
(D) 6 dollars

6. What can you NOT do in the cafe?

(A) bring snacks
(B) watch movies
(C) buy comic books
(D) read comic books

Part D. General Reading and Retelling

Our class has a new student. Her name is Vicky. She is from another country. She looks shy. I am shy, too. Vicky sits next to me. At first, we do not talk. She and I are very quiet. I want to talk to her. Then, I see a comic book in her bag. It is "Mayo's Hamburger." It is my favorite story! I talk to her. I ask, "Do you like Mayo's Hamburger?" She says, "Yes! It is my favorite story!" Now, Vicky and I love to be together. We talk about comics at lunch. After school, we go to a comic book store downtown. There we read many funny comic books. We laugh for hours. Vicky is my best friend!

7. What is the best title?

(A) My New Friend
(B) A Quiet Teacher
(C) Pets and Family
(D) Special Lunch Menu

8. How is Vicky at first?

(A) shy
(B) noisy
(C) funny
(D) happy

9. What is "Mayo's Hamburger"?

(A) a store
(B) a movie
(C) a TV show
(D) a comic book

10. What do Vicky and the writer do after school?

(A) watch a movie
(B) eat hamburgers
(C) read comic books
(D) go to a supermarket

Listening Practice

Listen and write.

MP3 S3-9

My New Best Friend

Our class has a new student. Her name is Vicky. She is from another country. She looks 1 ____________. I am shy, too. Vicky sits next to me. At first, we do not talk. She and I are very quiet. I want to talk to her. Then, I see a 2 ____________ book in her bag. It is “Mayo’s Hamburger.” It is my favorite story! I talk to her. I ask, “Do you like Mayo’s Hamburger?” She says, “Yes! It is my favorite story!” Now, Vicky and I love to be together. We talk about comics at lunch. After school, we go to a comic book store downtown. There we read many 3 ____________ comic books. We 4 ____________ for hours. Vicky is my best friend!

Word Bank

comic	shi
funny	shy
punny	camic
laf	laugh

Listen. Pause. Say each sentence.

MP3 S3-9G

Writing Practice

Write the words.

1

2

3

4

Write the words.

Summary

Vicky is a new student. She sits next to me. At first, we are quiet. But then we talk about ________________ comic books. We read them together. Now she is my best friend.

Word Puzzle

X	W	U	D	O	B	U	X	X	T	H	J	M	R	M
L	A	U	G	H	U	Y	G	J	O	Q	X	K	F	K
H	W	K	K	A	P	S	U	U	I	D	P	G	Y	I
C	O	M	I	C	B	O	O	K	J	O	V	G	L	M
S	O	I	D	L	M	F	S	V	O	R	K	A	P	P
G	I	K	J	M	O	M	T	X	R	K	R	D	A	Y
G	B	B	F	F	E	Z	H	Z	S	H	K	O	Z	L
W	I	A	U	H	T	F	P	F	M	J	P	F	J	I
D	C	C	N	V	H	Z	J	A	G	B	D	P	A	D
W	V	D	N	L	R	S	A	S	D	C	P	W	T	L
Y	A	K	Y	X	W	S	M	F	D	R	U	U	G	V
H	Q	T	I	I	D	W	S	R	V	I	N	X	R	L
E	U	P	O	B	B	Z	H	P	J	Z	V	O	E	R
I	N	Y	C	X	J	W	Y	W	B	Z	L	F	I	Q
N	M	E	E	Q	N	U	R	I	Q	S	C	E	R	C

Write the words. Then find them in the puzzle.

1 ______________ 2 ______________ 3 ______________ 4 ______________

Teacher's Book p.194

UNIT 10

Clubs Meet on Fridays

Are you in a school club?
Which club do you want to be in?

UNIT 10 Clubs Meet on Fridays

Miho loves Fridays. On Fridays, the school clubs meet. There are 20 clubs in her school. There is a magic club and a reading club. There is a science club and a math club. Miho is in the tennis club. She plays tennis. There are 15 students in the tennis club. There is just one leader. His name is Junha. He is a good tennis player. What do students do in the tennis club? First they run. They run in the gym for 10 minutes. They sweat a lot. Then, the students stand in a line. They watch Junha. Junha hits a ball. The other students follow. Then, Junha jumps from left to right. The other students follow. Miho likes jumping and hitting the ball. Fridays are great days!

New Words

tennis

sweat

leader

follow

Part A. Sentence Completion

1. What ________ they do on Fridays?

    (A) is
    (B) do
    (C) has
    (D) does

2. There is ________ leader.

    (A) one
    (B) two
    (C) many
    (D) more

Part B. Situational Writing

3.

On hot days, Junho ________ a lot.

(A) digs
(B) drops
(C) smiles
(D) sweats

4.

The kids are ________ in a line.

(A) cooking
(B) reading
(C) standing
(D) swimming

Come to the Taekwondo Club!

Friday 4PM - 6PM

In Taekwondo Club you can:

1. be healthy
2. make friends
3. feel great

For all people over 5 years old!

5. What is this poster about?

(A) a TV show
(B) a sports club
(C) a cooking club
(D) a clothing market

6. Who can NOT join the club?

(A) a baby
(B) a parent
(C) a teacher
(D) a student over 5

Part D. General Reading and Retelling

Miho loves Fridays. On Fridays, the school clubs meet. There are 20 clubs in her school. There is a magic club and a reading club. There is a science club and a math club. Miho is in the tennis club. She plays tennis. There are 15 students in the tennis club. There is just one leader. His name is Junha. He is a good tennis player. What do students do in the tennis club? First they run. They run in the gym for 10 minutes. They sweat a lot. Then, the students stand in a line. They watch Junha. Junha hits a ball. The other students follow. Then, Junha jumps from left to right. The other students follow. Miho likes jumping and hitting the ball. Fridays are great days!

7. What is the best title?
   (A) Learn to Jump
   (B) Miho the Leader
   (C) New Club Member
   (D) Miho's Club on Fridays

8. What club is Miho in?
   (A) the math club
   (B) the tennis club
   (C) the reading club
   (D) the science club

9. How many students are in Miho's club?
   (A) 10
   (B) 15
   (C) 20
   (D) 30

10. What does Miho's club do first?
   (A) hit balls
   (B) do magic
   (C) study math
   (D) run in the gym

Listening Practice

Listen and write.

MP3 S3-10

Clubs Meet on Fridays

Miho loves Fridays. On Fridays, the school clubs meet. There are 20 clubs in her school. There is a magic club and a reading club. There is a science club and a math club. Miho is in the [1] ______ club. She plays tennis. There are 15 students in the tennis club. There is just one [2] ______. His name is Junha. He is a good tennis player. What do students do in the tennis club? First they run. They run in the gym for 10 minutes. They [3] ______ a lot. Then, the students stand in a line. They watch Junha. Junha hits a ball. The other students follow. Then, Junha jumps from left to right. The other students [4] ______. Miho likes jumping and hitting the ball. Fridays are great days!

Word Bank

tennis	swet
reader	tenis
leader	follo
sweat	follow

Listen. Pause. Say each sentence.

MP3 S3-10G

Writing Practice

Write the words.

1 ☐☐☐☐☐☐

2 ☐☐☐☐☐

3 ☐☐☐☐☐☐

4 ☐☐☐☐☐☐

Write the words.

Summary

Miho is in the tennis club. Students run in the gym and stand in a line. The leader hits a ball and jumps. The students ________________ him.

Word Puzzle

M	L	E	A	D	E	R	E	H	X	R	J	K	U	G
K	I	Z	N	O	B	J	Y	G	K	G	F	Q	J	Z
M	I	H	W	K	L	C	B	O	F	N	O	T	W	L
R	O	I	A	V	Q	E	B	C	Z	O	L	R	M	M
R	Y	J	W	M	T	C	M	K	R	S	L	T	E	R
J	H	M	I	C	P	Z	P	R	K	V	O	G	G	D
E	J	C	R	N	U	W	N	T	H	D	W	L	S	Y
Q	Y	J	O	Z	F	S	J	E	M	Q	F	L	P	D
R	W	V	Y	B	S	W	J	N	O	O	U	N	R	R
J	H	L	J	D	Z	E	C	N	Y	O	E	E	V	Z
N	W	L	X	R	B	A	K	I	L	M	X	R	F	Q
C	W	C	Y	N	C	T	M	S	F	L	L	X	Y	W
V	D	M	Y	E	G	C	J	X	Z	Z	V	B	Z	D
X	I	X	U	A	Q	X	H	C	Z	B	S	P	L	X
V	I	M	Z	L	I	N	D	N	I	Q	W	B	X	R

Write the words. Then find them in the puzzle.

1 ______ 2 ______ 3 ______ 4 ______

Teacher's Book
p.198

UNIT 11

Word Game!

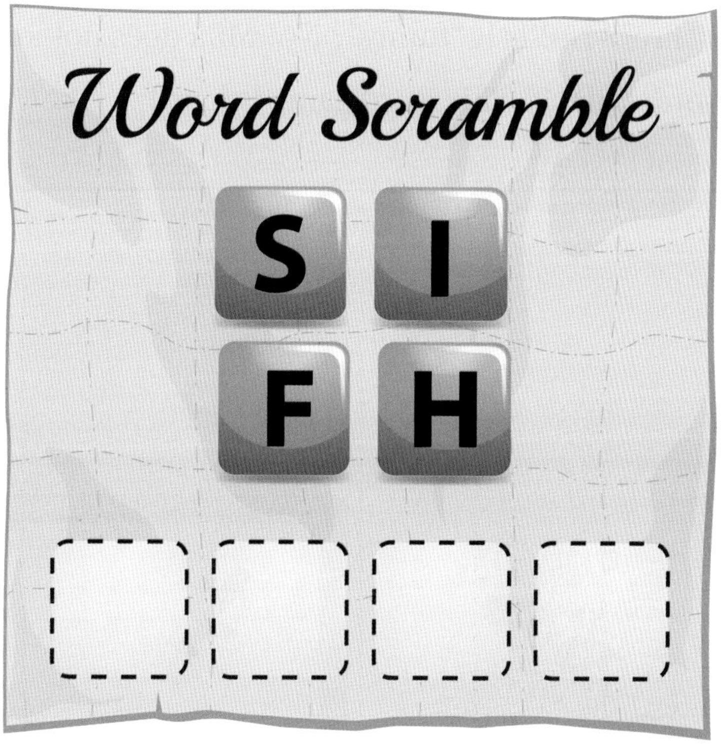

Look at the word game. What is the word?

UNIT 11 Word Game!

Let's play a word game! The rules are easy. Choose one word. After that, mix the letters! Mila chooses the word "happy." She mixes the letters. Now the word is "hpyap." She shows it to her friend. His name is Caleb. Caleb looks at the letters. He asks, "Is it "happy"?" Mila says, "Yes, it is. That is the right word!" Now, it is Caleb's turn. Caleb mixes the letters. He shows the letters to Mila. The letters are "fndrie." What is the word? Mila does not know. Is it "fire"? No! Is it "funny"? No! Mila does not know. She asks, "What is the word, Caleb?" This word game is hard!

New Words

word

mix

letter

choose

10 minutes

Part A. Sentence Completion

1. Let's ________ a word game!

(A) play
(B) plays
(C) playing
(D) be play

2. The dogs are waving ________ tails.

(A) it
(B) its
(C) their
(D) them

Part B. Situational Writing

3.

There are five ________ in this word.

(A) lines
(B) letters
(C) circles
(D) squares

4.

Mila ________ the chocolate muffin!

(A) plays
(B) draws
(C) sends
(D) chooses

Part C. Practical Reading and Retelling

Play these word games!

Game 1:
It sounds like "bake."
It is an animal.
It is long.
Here are the letters in the word: k-s-a-n-e

What is it?

Game 2:
Its first letter is "s."
You can eat it.
It has fresh vegetables.

What is it?

5. Game 1's answer is:

(A) sand
(B) koala
(C) candy
(D) snake

6. Game 2's answer is:

(A) fruit
(B) salad
(C) pasta
(D) cookie

Part D. General Reading and Retelling

Let's play a word game! The rules are easy. Choose one word. After that, mix the letters! Mila chooses the word "happy." She mixes the letters. Now the word is "hpyap." She shows it to her friend. His name is Caleb. Caleb looks at the letters. He asks, "Is it "happy"?" Mila says, "Yes, it is. That is the right word!" Now, it is Caleb's turn. Caleb mixes the letters. He shows the letters to Mila. The letters are "fndrie." What is the word? Mila does not know. Is it "fire"? No! Is it "funny"? No! Mila does not know. She asks, "What is the word, Caleb?" This word game is hard!

7. What is the best title?
   (A) How to Cook
   (B) Mix the Letters
   (C) School Talent Show
   (D) Rock, Paper, Scissors

8. What do Caleb and Mina play?
   (A) a word game
   (B) a math game
   (C) a baseball game
   (D) a computer game

9. What is Caleb's word?
   (A) fire
   (B) funny
   (C) friend
   (D) forest

10. What does Mila do?
   (A) go to sleep
   (B) make a fire
   (C) say the wrong word
   (D) choose the word "sun"

Listening Practice

Listen and write.

MP3 S3-11

Word Game!

Let's play a [1] ________ game! The rules are easy. Choose one word. After that, [2] ________ the letters! Mila [3] ________ the word "happy." She mixes the letters. Now the word is "hpyap." She shows it to her friend. His name is Caleb. Caleb looks at the letters. He asks, "Is it "happy"?" Mila says, "Yes, it is. That is the right word!" Now, it is Caleb's turn. Caleb mixes the letters. He shows the [4] ________ to Mila. The letters are "fndrie." What is the word? Mila does not know. Is it "fire"? No! Is it "funny"? No! Mila does not know. She asks, "What is the word, Caleb?" This word game is hard!

Word Bank

chooses	letters
word	mix
werd	ledders
choozes	miks

Listen. Pause. Say each sentence.

MP3 S3-11G

Writing Practice

Write the words.

1 ☐☐☐☐

2 ☐☐☐

3 ☐☐☐☐☐☐

4 ☐☐☐☐☐☐

Write the words.

Summary

Here is a word game. Choose one word. Mix up the ________________.

Show the letters to your friend. Your friend guesses the word.

Word Puzzle

W	B	R	Y	A	T	I	X	C	C	H	O	O	S	E
T	P	F	X	W	X	O	K	X	O	G	U	I	G	V
Y	X	C	Z	F	R	C	J	P	O	S	Q	T	L	G
J	U	M	F	M	I	X	U	D	J	A	W	R	D	M
C	B	P	C	H	U	B	D	L	E	T	T	E	R	C
O	V	A	T	O	P	W	W	Y	O	W	T	J	L	A
V	V	N	A	E	W	L	V	C	N	A	T	H	C	F
Y	S	I	Y	F	S	M	S	X	X	V	W	T	S	R
V	I	Z	S	W	P	D	Q	G	X	D	W	G	B	B
G	M	K	V	G	J	A	Z	F	A	D	W	W	I	B
Z	U	C	A	J	Y	R	M	T	B	Q	F	N	A	W
L	A	I	E	E	Q	W	Z	M	K	T	O	N	W	M
T	T	P	A	Y	Q	W	L	H	C	F	O	K	L	N
C	E	Q	S	K	K	H	Q	D	D	Y	I	I	Q	K
Z	T	M	V	T	W	W	O	R	D	I	F	S	O	D

Write the words. Then find them in the puzzle.

1 ____________

2 ____________

3 ____________

4 ____________

Teacher's Book
p.202

UNIT 12

Weekend Fun

Think! You go to your friend's house.
What do you do there?

UNIT 12 Weekend Fun

Jake and Kareem are best friends. They have fun on Saturdays. Jake stays at Kareem's house often. And Kareem stays at Jake's house often. They have pizza and salad for dinner. They like a lot of cheese on the pizza. After dinner, they watch a movie. They eat popcorn. Then, they play video games. Jake is good at "Break King." Kareem is good at "Dance Star." At 9 PM, they wash and go to bed. In the morning, they eat cereal. Kareem puts bananas in his cereal. Jake does not like bananas. What do they do after breakfast? They go out and play soccer. Jake is good at kicking the ball! They play for one hour. Jake and Kareem love the weekend!

New Words

fun

salad

be good at

weekend

10 minutes

Part A. Sentence Completion

1. Jake and Kareem play table tennis ________ 2 hours.

(A) at
(B) to
(C) on
(D) for

2. How can you be so good at ________?

(A) draw
(B) draws
(C) to draw
(D) drawing

Part B. Situational Writing

3.

We are having a ________ for fun.

(A) campfire
(B) cup of tea
(C) pillow fight
(D) lunch break

4.

This soda has ________ sugar in it.

(A) no
(B) many
(C) a lot of
(D) a little bit of

Part C. Practical Reading and Retelling

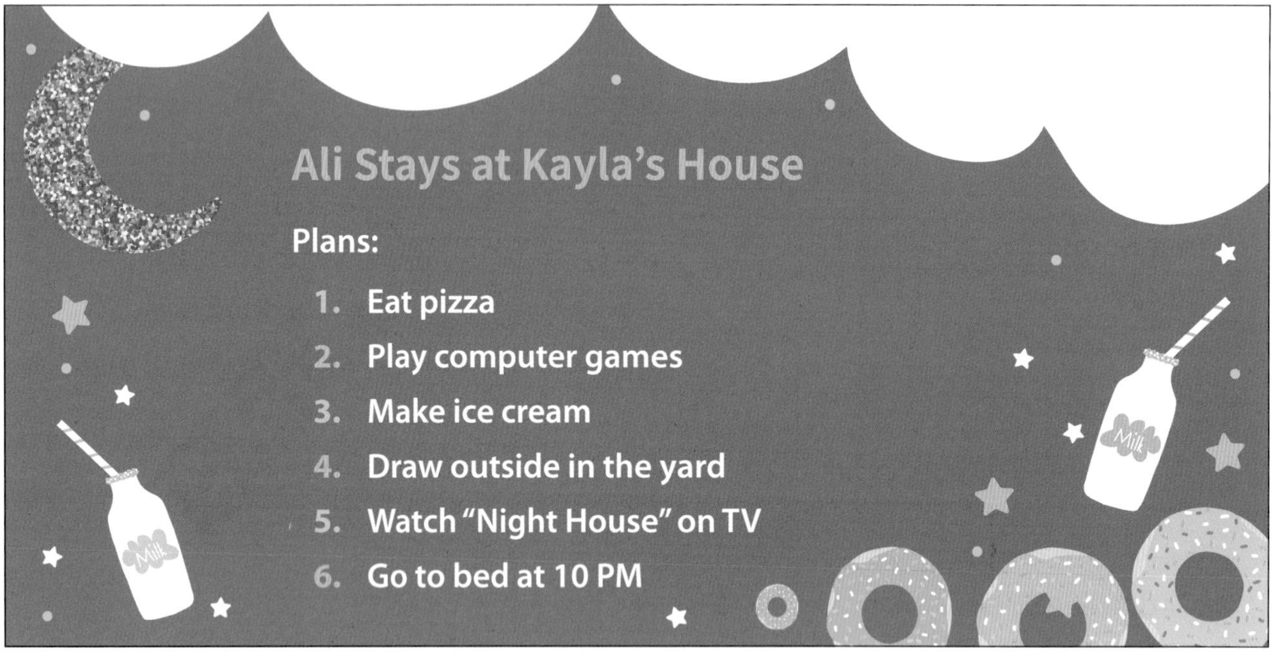

5. What do Ali and Kayla NOT do?

   (A) watch TV
   (B) eat burgers
   (C) draw outside
   (D) make ice cream

6. When do Ali and Kayla go to sleep?

   (A) at 9
   (B) at 10
   (C) at 11
   (D) at 12

Part D. General Reading and Retelling

Jake and Kareem are best friends. They have fun on Saturdays. Jake stays at Kareem's house often. And Kareem stays at Jake's house often. They have pizza and salad for dinner. They like a lot of cheese on the pizza. After dinner, they watch a movie. They eat popcorn. Then, they play video games. Jake is good at "Break King." Kareem is good at "Dance Star." At 9 PM, they wash and go to bed. In the morning, they eat cereal. Kareem puts bananas in his cereal. Jake does not like bananas. What do they do after breakfast? They go out and play soccer. Jake is good at kicking the ball! They play for one hour. Jake and Kareem love the weekend!

7. What is the best title?

   (A) Sleeping at School
   (B) Jake Makes a Pizza
   (C) Kareem Wakes Up at 9
   (D) Jake and Kareem's Weekend

8. What do Jake and Kareem have for dinner?

   (A) pizza
   (B) cereal
   (C) popcorn
   (D) cheese cake

9. What does Jake NOT like?

   (A) pizza
   (B) cereal
   (C) popcorn
   (D) bananas

10. What is Kareem good at?

   (A) driving a car
   (B) making movies
   (C) playing "Dance Star"
   (D) playing "Break King"

Listening Practice

Listen and write.

MP3 S3-12

Weekend Fun

Jake and Kareem are best friends. They have [1] on Saturdays. Jake stays at Kareem's house often. And Kareem stays at Jake's house often. They have pizza and [2] for dinner. They like a lot of cheese on the pizza. After dinner, they watch a movie. They eat popcorn. Then, they play video games. Jake is good at "Break King." Kareem is [3] "Dance Star." At 9 PM, they wash and go to bed. In the morning, they eat cereal. Kareem puts bananas in his cereal. Jake does not like bananas. What do they do after breakfast? They go out and play soccer. Jake is good at kicking the ball! They play for one hour. Jake and Kareem love the [4] !

Word Bank

pun	goodat
wekend	fun
weekend	good at
salad	sallad

Listen. Pause. Say each sentence.

MP3 S3-12G

Writing Practice

Write the words.

1

2

3

4

Write the words.

Summary

On Saturdays, Jake goes to Kareem's house. Kareem goes to Jake's house. They ________________ pizza and salad. They watch movies, play video games, and play soccer.

Word Puzzle

V	S	W	R	J	F	F	B	Y	L	R	J	T	T	Z
H	J	E	R	T	X	U	A	C	W	G	O	P	L	M
M	R	E	W	I	Y	N	O	T	G	F	U	L	O	R
V	N	K	R	Z	E	W	X	V	H	V	V	I	E	I
N	B	E	G	O	O	D	A	T	Y	T	S	S	B	C
Z	V	N	X	A	V	E	N	O	W	Q	V	B	N	H
R	X	D	F	X	M	E	Z	L	H	A	L	K	B	A
G	B	P	L	V	S	O	S	I	V	J	S	J	Y	B
J	V	J	T	T	C	G	J	D	A	M	A	H	Q	W
X	X	S	D	T	S	Y	A	J	X	E	L	M	C	N
P	E	H	Y	P	B	B	X	I	K	C	A	W	R	P
D	C	O	L	S	Z	R	G	Q	U	M	D	W	L	V
M	L	F	J	E	M	T	S	W	C	W	Z	F	G	R
C	M	Y	A	I	O	V	S	G	B	V	G	L	R	B
G	I	W	S	T	V	V	H	N	U	T	K	Y	F	A

Write the words. Then find them in the puzzle.

1 ______________

2 ______________

3 ______________

4 ______________

CHAPTER REVIEW

Match the pictures to the correct words.

Teacher's Book p.206

be good at
choose
comic book
follow
fun
funny
laugh
leader
letter
mix
salad
shy
sweat
tennis
weekend
word

ANSWERS

CHAPTER 1 | School Activity p.10

UNIT 1	1 (A)	2 (B)	3 (B)	4 (D)	5 (A)	6 (C)	7 (D)	8 (B)	9 (B)	10 (C)
S3-1	1 kind		2 play		3 good at		4 bad at			
p.11	1 kind		2 be good at		3 play		4 be bad at		am bad at	
	1 kind		2 be good at		3 play		4 be bad at			
UNIT 2	1 (B)	2 (A)	3 (A)	4 (C)	5 (C)	6 (D)	7 (D)	8 (B)	9 (B)	10 (C)
S3-2	1 paintings		2 gallery		3 artwork		4 touch			
p.19	1 painting		2 gallery		3 touch		4 artwork		paintings	
	1 painting		2 gallery		3 touch		4 artwork			
UNIT 3	1 (B)	2 (A)	3 (B)	4 (B)	5 (C)	6 (C)	7 (A)	8 (B)	9 (A)	10 (D)
S3-3	1 cucumbers		2 sour		3 pour		4 dressing			
p.27	1 cucumber		2 sour		3 dressing		4 pour		pour	
	1 cucumber		2 sour		3 dressing		4 pour			
UNIT 4	1 (D)	2 (A)	3 (B)	4 (B)	5 (D)	6 (B)	7 (D)	8 (A)	9 (D)	10 (C)
S3-4	1 buddy		2 street		3 owners		4 town			
p.35	1 buddy		2 street dog		3 owner		4 town		street	
	1 buddy		2 street dog		3 owner		4 town			

CHAPTER 2 | School Festival p.44

UNIT 5	1 (C)	2 (A)	3 (D)	4 (A)	5 (D)	6 (C)	7 (B)	8 (B)	9 (D)	10 (A)
S3-5	1 aquarium		2 mermaid		3 costumes		4 wave			
p.45	1 aquarium		2 mermaid		3 costume		4 wave		aquarium	
	1 aquarium		2 mermaid		3 costume		4 wave			
UNIT 6	1 (A)	2 (A)	3 (B)	4 (B)	5 (A)	6 (C)	7 (B)	8 (A)	9 (D)	10 (D)
S3-6	1 fair		2 kings		3 queens		4 crown			
p.53	1 book fair		2 crown		3 king		4 queen		book fair	
	1 book fair		2 crown		3 king		4 queen			
UNIT 7	1 (B)	2 (A)	3 (B)	4 (D)	5 (B)	6 (A)	7 (B)	8 (A)	9 (A)	10 (D)
S3-7	1 fast		2 race		3 finish		4 winners			
p.61	1 fast		2 race		3 winner		4 finish		race	
	1 fast		2 race		3 winner		4 finish			
UNIT 8	1 (D)	2 (D)	3 (A)	4 (A)	5 (C)	6 (D)	7 (C)	8 (C)	9 (A)	10 (D)
S3-8	1 market		2 sell		3 expensive		4 board			
p.69	1 market		2 sell		3 expensive		4 board game		market	
	1 market		2 sell		3 expensive		4 board game			

CHAPTER 3 | Fun with Friends p.78

UNIT 9	1 (B)	2 (A)	3 (C)	4 (D)	5 (B)	6 (B)	7 (A)	8 (A)	9 (D)	10 (C)
S3-9	1 shy		2 comic		3 funny		4 laugh			
p.79	1 shy		2 comic book		3 funny		4 laugh		funny	
	1 shy		2 comic book		3 funny		4 laugh			
UNIT 10	1 (B)	2 (A)	3 (D)	4 (C)	5 (B)	6 (A)	7 (D)	8 (B)	9 (B)	10 (D)
S3-10	1 tennis		2 leader		3 sweat		4 follow			
p.87	1 tennis		2 sweat		3 leader		4 follow		follow	
	1 tennis		2 sweat		3 leader		4 follow			
UNIT 11	1 (A)	2 (C)	3 (B)	4 (D)	5 (D)	6 (B)	7 (B)	8 (A)	9 (C)	10 (C)
S3-11	1 word		2 mix		3 chooses		4 letters			
p.95	1 word		2 mix		3 letter		4 choose		letters	
	1 word		2 mix		3 letter		4 choose			
UNIT 12	1 (D)	2 (D)	3 (C)	4 (C)	5 (B)	6 (B)	7 (D)	8 (A)	9 (D)	10 (C)
S3-12	1 fun		2 salad		3 good at		4 weekend			
p.103	1 fun		2 salad		3 be good at		4 weekend		have	
	1 fun		2 salad		3 be good at		4 weekend			